A VISIT TO

Cambodia

REVISED AND UPDATED

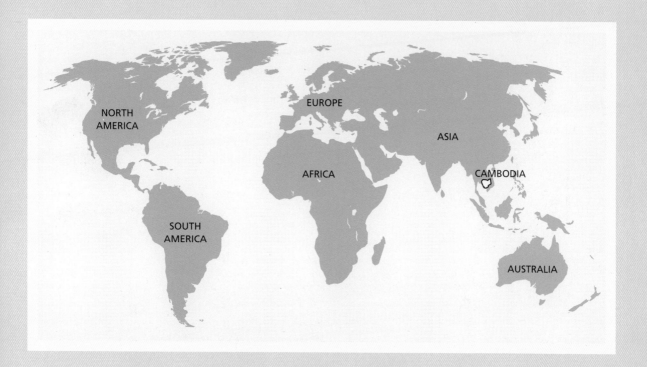

Rob Alcraft

Heinemann Library
Chicago, Illinois

© 1999, 2009 Heinemann Library
a division of Pearson Inc.
Chicago, Illinois

Customer Service 888-454-2279
Visit our website at www.heinemannraintree.com

Designed by Joanna Hinton-Malivoire
Printed in China by South China Printing Company Limited

13 12 11 10 09
10 9 8 7 6 5 4 3 2 1

New edition ISBN-10:1-4329-1277-1 (hardcover), 1-4329-1296-8 (paperback)
New edition ISBN-13: 978-1-4329-1277-2 (hardcover), 978-1-4329-1296-3 (paperback)

The Library of Congress has cataloged the first edition as follows:
Alcraft, Rob, 1966–
    A visit to Cambodia. – (Heinemann first library)
    1. Cambodia – Juvenile literature
    I. Title II. Cambodia
    959.6

Acknowledgments
The author and publishers are grateful to the following for permission to reproduce photographs:
© Alamy pp. **7** (Bruce Percy), **14** (Tony Clements); © Colourific! Michael Yamashita pp. **13**, **16** (Catherine Karnow), **27**; © Getty Images p. **19** (The Image Bank/Nicholas Pitt); Hutchison Library pp. **10** (Sarah Murray), **28** (Nigel Sitwell); Link pp. **24** (Sue Carpenter), **26** (Jan Knapik); © Panos Pictures pp. **5** (Nic Dunlop), **8** (Jim Holmes), **18**, **20** (Jon Spaull), **21**, **22**, **23** (Irene Slegt); © Robert Harding Picture Library p. **24** (Gavin Hellier); © Still Pictures p. **6** (Gilles Martin); © Telegraph Colour Library p. **29** (Masterfile); © Trip pp. **9** (A. Gasson), **11** (B. A. Dixie Dean), **12** (Ask Images), **15** (F. Nichols), **17**.

Cover photograph reproduced with permission of © Masterfile (Lonely Planet).

Every effort has been made to contact copyright holders of any material reproduced in this book. Any omissions will be rectified in subsequent printings if notice is given to the publisher.

Contents

Any words appearing in bold, **like this**, are explained in the Glossary.

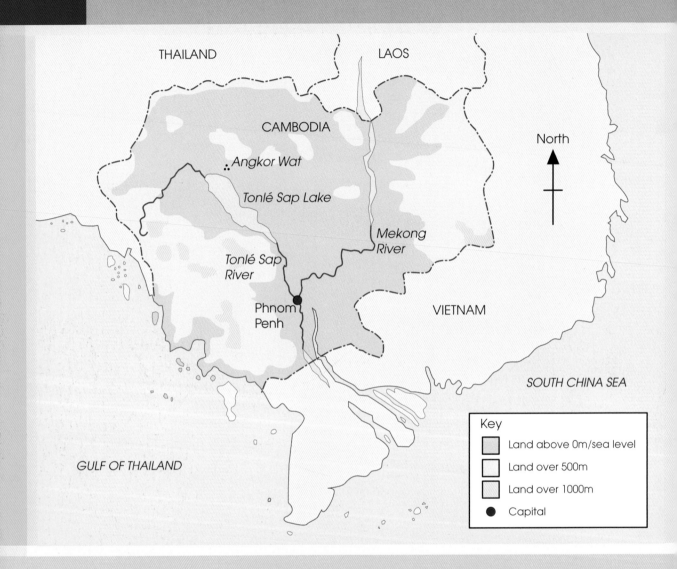

Cambodia is in **Southeast Asia**. The land is very flat and very green.

There are two big rivers in Cambodia. They are the Tonlé Sap and the Mekong.

Cambodia is a land of rice fields and rivers.

Cambodia has thick forests. Tall trees grow as high as a 12-story building. Leopards, elephants, and bears live in the forests.

In Cambodia, winds called **monsoons** bring heavy rain. For four or five months, it rains every day. The rain makes the **crops** grow.

Monsoon clouds bring heavy rain to water the rice fields.

 # Landmarks

Angkor Wat is a 900-year-old **temple**. It is built from blocks of stone that fit together perfectly. Angkor Wat was once part of a great city.

Tonlé Sap Lake can cover more than 4,600 square miles in the rainy season.

There is a huge lake in the middle of Cambodia. It is called the Tonlé Sap Lake. It is wide and shallow and full of fish.

Homes

Most people in Cambodia live in the country. They build their homes on **stilts** to keep them dry and cool. They make the roofs from **palm tree** leaves.

There is one big city in Cambodia. It is the **capital** city, which is called Phnom Penh. Families in the city live in small houses or apartments.

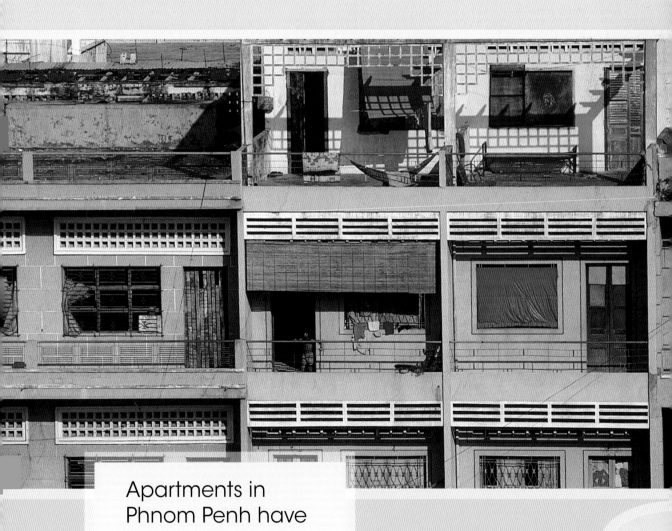

Apartments in Phnom Penh have one or two rooms.

Food

Cambodians eat with **chopsticks**. They eat lots of rice. Sometimes a sauce of peanuts and fish, or salad with garlic and mint, is added to the rice.

People buy fish in busy markets.

Fish is a favorite Cambodian food. The fish is grilled, wrapped in lettuce leaves, and dipped in a spicy sauce.

Clothes

Cambodian clothes are light and cool. Men and women wear a cloth that they wrap around them like a skirt, or they wear pants. On top they wear a shirt.

Some young Cambodian men become **Buddhist monks**. They wear bright orange robes and shave their heads. They must keep 227 promises in order to be a monk.

Work

When the **monsoon** rains come, **buffalo** pull farmers' **plows** through the fields. Then the farmers plant rice. Each rice plant is pushed into the wet ground by hand.

Cambodia does not have large factories. Many people work in small shops. They repair and make things. Fishing is important work, too.

Transportation

Most Cambodians travel by bicycle, motorcycle, and special bicycle taxi.

Some Cambodian children go to school by boat.

For long journeys, Cambodians take the bus or go by boat. People travel by boat on the big rivers and on the huge Tonlé Sap Lake.

Language

Cambodians speak a language called Khmer. Khmer has its own alphabet. The writing goes from left to right, but there are no spaces between the words.

Khmer has 100 different words for "rice."
There are two words for "yes." Women
use one of the "yes" words, and men use
the other.

School

At school, Cambodian children learn to read and write Khmer. They learn math with Khmer numbers. Cambodian children also learn English.

It can cost a lot of money to go to school. There was a war in Cambodia for more than 20 years. Many schools were destroyed during the war.

Cambodians enjoy going to **festivals**. The whole family will put on their best clothes and visit their local **temple**.

Many Cambodian children help their parents in their free time. They help grow rice, or they sell sweets and fruit to make money.

Celebrations

Cambodians celebrate the Khmer New Year in April. People give each other presents or new clothes, and they take gifts to their local **temple**.

During the **monsoon** rains, the big
Tonlé Sap River gets so full that it
flows backward. When this happens,
Cambodians have their Water **Festival**.

The Arts

Royal dance is a very old Cambodian art. Dancers wear beautiful costumes. The dances tell stories of love and war.

There are many old **carvings** in Cambodia. Today, artists still carve beautiful images of the **Buddha**.

Fact File

Name	The full name of Cambodia is the Kingdom of Cambodia.
Capital	The **capital** city is Phnom Penh.
Language	Most Cambodians speak Khmer.
Population	There are nearly 14 million people living in Cambodia.
Money	Cambodians use money called riel.
Religions	Most Cambodians follow **Buddhism**.
Products	Cambodia produces rice, fish, rubber, paper, and wood.

Words you can learn

joom reab suor (JEWM RE-a SUE-o)	hello
bat (BAH)	yes (said by men)
jas (JAHS)	yes (said by women)
te	no
ar kun (R KUN)	thank you
suom (SUE-um)	please
pee	two
bram	five
bram-pee	seven

Glossary

Buddha a man who lived long ago whose teachings are followed by Buddhists

Buddhist follower of the teachings of the Buddha. The religion is called Buddhism.

buffalo a large, cow-like animal often used in Asia to do the work of a tractor

capital an important city where a country's government has its headquarters

carving picture or sculpture cut from stone or wood

chopsticks a pair of smooth sticks held in one hand and used to lift food to the mouth

crop a plant, such as rice, that is grown for food

festival party held by a whole town or country

monk young man who spends time learning about a religion such as Buddhism. Women who do this are called nuns.

monsoon a name for a season with lots of rain

palm tree a tree with large, narrow leaves that spread out at the top of a long trunk

plow a machine used to break up the soil before seeds are planted

Southeast Asia the part of Asia that includes Cambodia, Laos, Burma, Thailand, Vietnam, Malaysia, and some other island countries such as the Philippines and Indonesia

stilts supports that are like legs

temple a special place of worship for Buddhists

unique different in a special way

Index